Published by Christian Focus Publications Ltd
Geanies House, Fearn, Tain, Ross-shire IV20 1TW www.christianfocus.com

Copyright © John Brown Brian Wright
ISBN: 978-1-5271-1169-1

This edition published in 2024
Cover illustration and internal illustrations by Lisa Flanagan
Cover and internal design by Lisa Flanagan
Printed and bound by Imprint, India

All rights reserved. No part of this publication may be reproduced, stored in a retrieval system, or transmitted, in any form, by any means, electronic, mechanical, photocopying, recording or otherwise without the prior permission of the publisher or a licence permitting restricted copying. In the U.K. such licences are issued by the Copyright Licensing Agency, 4 Battlebridge Lane, London, SE1 2HX. www.cla.co.uk

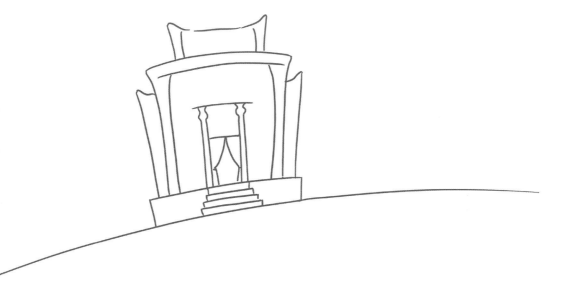

Zechariah's encouragement

John Brown
Brian Wright

Long ago God's people **stopped rebuilding** God's temple. So the Lord sent the prophet **Zechariah** to encourage them.

"Return to Me, and I will return to you!"

says the Lord of Hosts.
Then the Lord showed Zechariah **eight visions** in **one night** to encourage the people to **finish the temple** and **live right**.

In the **first vision** Zechariah saw several riders returned from patrol.

"The earth is at **peace**,"
a rider declares.
Then the Lord spoke **kind**
and **comforting** words.

"I **love** Jerusalem and have **chosen** her as My own!"

"I will **restore** the city,
rebuild the temple,
bless the towns,
and **comfort** the country."

In the **second vision** Zechariah saw four **horns**.

The angel explained, "These horns represent the **nations**, which scattered Judah, Israel, and Jerusalem."

"But God will **destroy** those who hurt His people."

"He will **tear down** those who scattered Israel."

The Lord of Hosts would **defeat** Israel's enemies, so God's people should not be afraid to **finish** God's temple.

In the **third vision** Zechariah saw someone **measuring Jerusalem.**
"Some day Jerusalem will be so big she'll outgrow her walls!"
"**God** will be a wall of **fire** around her and the **glory** in her midst."

"Come home, my people!
Sing for joy and be glad!
You are the **apple** of **My eye**,
and I am coming to live with you!
Many **nations** will become
My people in that day!"

The **fourth vision** showed Satan accusing **Joshua** the priest.

But God said, "This one is a branch **snatched** from the **fire**."
"Take off his **filthy clothes** and give him **new garments**."
"Joshua, I have **removed** your **sins**. Now **walk** in My ways to **serve** Me in My temple."

"I will **purify Israel** like I did Joshua, and I will send My servant, '**the Branch**'."

"I will **remove** everyone's **sins** in a single day."
"And My people will sit with their **friends** under their **vines** and **fig trees**."

After four visions, Zechariah was **exhausted!**
So the angel had to wake him for the **fifth.**

Zechariah saw a gold **lampstand**
with two **olive trees.**
These meant that **God's power**
would rebuild God's temple.

"Not by might, not by power, but by **My Spirit**," says the Lord of Hosts.
"Don't be sad that the temple looks small now.
The Lord knows all and will finish the work."

Zechariah's **sixth vision** showed a large **scroll**, **flying** through the air, with writing on both sides.

"Those who steal or swear falsely or **break** His **commandments** will be banished!"
"For God expects His people to **obey Him!**"

The **seventh vision** showed two winged-women carrying away a wicked lady in a large **basket.**

"This is **Wickedness**," the angel explained, "whom God is sending away to **Babylon.**" For God expects His people to **remove sin** from their lives **and wickedness** from their land.

The **last vision** showed **four chariots**
coming down from two bronze mountains.

The angel said, "These are **four spirits**
from heaven sent to earth by God."
The Lord added, "The chariots going north
will vent my anger against those nations
who hurt my people."

After the **visions,**
the Lord gave Zechariah **instructions.**

"Crown **Joshua** the priest and tell him:
'A **Branch** will come and establish the
temple of the Lord.'
He will combine the offices of
priest and **king.**"

Two years later, God's people asked if they should still fast and be sad on the date that Jerusalem had been destroyed.
Zechariah said that what pleases God is not religious rituals but **right living**.

"Act **justly**. Show **mercy**. Be **kind**."
"Do not mistreat widows, orphans, foreigners, or poor people. Do not plot harm against each other."
"Do not plug your ears or harden your heart when God speaks to you."

"It is because your ancestors did these bad things that I sent Israel into captivity and made its land desolate."
Then Zechariah shared how the Lord intended to **bless** His people and turn their fasting into feasting!

This is what the Lord of Hosts says:
"I love Jerusalem! I will live there,
so it will be called the **Faithful City**
and the **Holy Mountain.**"
"**Children** will **play** in her streets
while adults walk and sit."
"**Water** will be ample, **vines** full,
crops rich, and everyone **prosperous.**"

"So do not mourn—finish the temple and celebrate!"
"Speak **truth**. Do **right**.
Love **honesty**, **justice**, and **peace**."
"I will **rescue** My people and bring them **home**."
"Other nations will come to Jerusalem to **worship** as well,
and I will **bless** them and give them **peace**."

"I am also angry with **Israel's leaders** for being **bad shepherds.**"
To make His point, God made **Zechariah** become a **shepherd** for a season, to act out the wrong things Israel's leaders had done. He broke a staff named **Favor** and another named **Union** to show how Israel's leaders had cursed and divided the nation.

He threw away the **insulting wages** he was paid to show how Israel had ungratefully insulted God. Then Zechariah left the flock with a **worthless shepherd**, like God had done with Israel for a time. But God promised to send a better leader—
the best ever!

"Rejoice, My people! Your king is coming to save you!"
"He is **righteous** and **humble**, riding on a donkey."
"Your king will bring peace and reign over the earth."
"He will free those in bondage and make them safe."

The Lord will deliver His people from their enemies.
He will **save** His people like a shepherd rescues his sheep.
The fields will **flourish.** The land will be lush.
The people will thrive. The children will be happy.
All will be well for everyone always.

God's **final** message to Zechariah was how He would save His people from **both** their enemies and **from** their sins.

This is what the Lord says, the creator of heavens and earth. "When the nations attack Jerusalem, I will defend her and destroy them." "On that day, the weakest person will be as mighty as King David, for the angel of the Lord **will go** before them."

"I will pour out a spirit of **grace** and **prayer** on Jerusalem."
"They will look on **Me whom they have pierced** and mourn for Him as for a firstborn son who has died."

This **prophecy** was **fulfilled** five hundred years later when **Jesus** Christ **died** on the **cross!**
God gave His people a spirit of **repentance** to pray for **forgiveness** and embrace **Jesus** as their **Savior.**

God would not only **forgive** but also purify His people.
"I will open a fountain to **cleanse** My people from all their sins and impurity."
"I will remove the worship of idols throughout the land and cause their names to be forgotten."
"I will likewise remove false prophets and make them ashamed to deceive people anymore."

"Strike down the shepherd
and the sheep will be scattered."
"But I will preserve a remnant. I will **refine**
them like silver and **purify** them like gold."
"They will call on my name,
and I will **answer** them."
"I will say, 'These are my people,'
and they will say, "The Lord is our God.'"

God's final message to Zechariah describes the time when the **Lord** will **reign** forever from a **new Jerusalem** on a **new earth.**

"It will **always be light**, with no darkness to fear."

"**Waters of life** will flow freely from Jerusalem."
"God's people will be **completely safe** forever.
"The Lord will be **king of all the earth,**
and only He will be worshiped."

"Everything will be **holy to the Lord**,
and everything will be **sacred**."
"Everyone will be able to **approach God** freely,
for everyone will be **holy**."
"No one mean and nothing evil will be there."
"Only **God's people** will live with the
Lord of hosts in that day."

Israel heard Zechariah's words. They **repented** of their sins, **returned** to God, and **rebuilt** the temple.
God wants us to listen to Zechariah as well.
God loves us and sent Jesus to save us.

Jesus is the priestly Branch, who removes all our sins.

Jesus is the humble King, who entered Jerusalem on a donkey.

Jesus is the God-man, who was pierced for us.

Jesus is the Shepherd, who was struck down for us.

And Jesus is the Lord, who is coming to rule the earth.

So we should tell God we're sorry for our sins and ask Jesus to save us.

We should stop disobeying God and do good and be kind.

And when we get discouraged and distracted and doubt, we should remember what God has in store for His people.

Because of Jesus, we will **live with the Lord** in **holiness, blessedness,** and **peace** forever and **forever** and forever.

Christian Focus Publications publishes books for adults and children under its four main imprints: Christian Focus, CF4K, Mentor, and Christian Heritage. Our books reflect our conviction that God's Word is reliable and that Jesus is the way to know Him, and live for ever with Him.

Our children's publication list covers pre-school to early teens. We also publish personal and family devotionals, biographies and inspirational stories that children will love.

From pre-school board books to teenage apologetics, we have it covered!

Christian Focus Publications Ltd,
Geanies House, Fearn, Ross-shire,
IV20 1TW, Scotland,
United Kingdom.
www.christianfocus.com

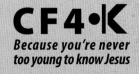